# Who Is JESUS?

Lois Rock

Pauline
BOOKS & MEDIA
Boston

*Nihil Obstat:*
Rev. John L. Sullivan, S.S.L.
*Imprimatur:*
✠ Seán Cardinal O'Malley, O.F.M. Cap.
Archbishop of Boston
June 8, 2006

**Library of Congress Cataloging-in-Publication Data**

Rock, Lois, 1953-
   [Tell me about Jesus]
   Who is Jesus? / Lois Rock.
      p. cm.
   Originally published: Tell me about Jesus. Oxford, England : Lion Hudson, 2006.
   Includes index.
   ISBN 0-8198-8313-1
   1. Jesus Christ—Biography—Juvenile literature.  I. Title.
   BT302.R677 2007
   232.9'01—dc22
   [B]
                                        2006017749

"P" and PAULINE are registered trademarks of the Daughters of St. Paul.

Original edition published in English under the title *Tell Me About Jesus* by Lion Hudson plc, Oxford, England.

Copyright © Lion Hudson plc, 2006

Text copyright © 2006, Lois Rock

The moral rights of the author have been asserted.

First North American edition, 2007

Published by Pauline Books & Media, 50 Saint Paul's Avenue, Boston, MA 02130-3491. www.pauline.org

Printed in China.

Pauline Books & Media is the publishing house of the Daughters of St. Paul, an international congregation of women religious serving the Church with the communications media.   ·

1 2 3 4 5 6 7 8 9          11 10 09 08 07

The Scripture quotations contained herein are from the *New Revised Standard Version Bible: Catholic Edition*, copyright © 1989, 1993, Division of Christian Education of the National Council of the Churches of Christ in the United States of America. Used by permission. All rights reserved.

**Picture acknowledgements:**

Picture research courtesy of Zooid Pictures Limited and Lion Hudson.

Front cover: Main image by Gail Newey; side images from top by the Bodleian Library, University of Oxford, and David Townsend.

Back cover: Top image by Gail Newey; images below by John Williams.

**All illustrations, unless otherwise noted below, by Gail Newey.**

AKG-Images: pp. 7b, 27t (Erich Lessing).

Alamy: pp. 23t (Tim Graham); 23b (Christine Osborne/World Religions Photo Library).

David Alexander: p. 31b.

Bodleian Library, University of Oxford: pp. 8b, 16, 40.

Bridgeman Art Library: pp. 41b (National Museum of Ireland, Dublin, Ireland); 42t.

Corbis UK Ltd.: pp. 6 (Chris Hellier); 11t, 12 (Christie's Images); 15b, 39 (Arte & Immagini srl); 25t (Hanan Isachar); 30 (Elio Ciol); 32 (Shai Ginott); 34 (Reuters); 36t (Araldo de Luca); 43 (Craig Aurness); 44 (Richard T. Nowitz).

Empics: p. 45b (Jorge Saenz/Associated Press).

Focoltone International Ltd.: pp. 2, 33.

Lion Hudson: pp. 7t, 15t, 19tr, 24b, 45t (Jacqueline Crawford); 10t, 21t, 27b (David Townsend); 10b, 13b, 20t, 28b, 36b, 41t (John Williams).

PA Photos: p. 37b (Johnny Green).

Zev Radovan, www.BibleLandPictures.com: pp. 11b, 24t, 26t.

Rex Nicholls: pp. 8t, 19l, 20b, 35t, 35b, 38.

John Rylands University Library of Manchester: p. 9b (reproduced by courtesy of the Director and University Librarian).

Superstock Ltd.: p. 28t (3LH-Fine Art).

(r = right; l = left; t = top; b = bottom)

# Contents

1 Jesus: The Son of God

2 Learning about Jesus

3 Jesus' Birth: Matthew's Story

4 Jesus' Birth: Luke's Story

5 Jesus' New Beginning

6 Jesus' Message

7 Turn Away from Your Sins

8 God's Forgiveness

9 The Right Way to Live

10 God's Children

11 God's Power on Earth

12 Friends of Jesus

13 Who Will Follow Jesus?

14 Who Is Jesus?

15 Jesus in Jerusalem

16 The Last Supper

17 Jesus on Trial

18 The Crucifixion

19 The Resurrection

20 The Followers of Jesus

21 Index

21 Look It Up

# Jesus: The Son of God

Jesus is often called "Christ." This Greek title has the same meaning as the Hebrew word "messiah": God's chosen king.

JESUS IS THE MAN whose life and teachings are at the heart of the Christian faith. He lived around 2000 years ago, in a land that the Romans had made part of their empire. However, his people, the Jews, had remained fiercely loyal to their own faith and traditions. Jesus' own message was rooted in that faith.

## The Jewish People

The Jewish people traced their beginnings to a man named Abraham. They believed that God had promised him that he would be the father of a great nation—one that would bring God's blessing to the world.

## Moses, the Law and the Covenant

The years went by and Abraham's descendants faced hard times. In the end, they became slaves of the powerful king of Egypt. It was only when God chose a man named Moses to lead them to a new land that they had any chance of being free.

Through Moses, God made an agreement, or covenant, with the people. They must worship God and obey God's laws, and God would bless them.

## A Kingdom and Its Prophets

The people faced many difficulties making the new land their home. Many generations passed before a shepherd boy-turned-fighter defeated all the nation's enemies and made himself king. The king's name was David, and he began building a new city called Jerusalem. His son, Solomon, built a wonderful temple there.

After Solomon's death, more troubles came upon the nation. Time and again they were defeated. The Jewish people began to hope that the words of their prophets would come true: that God would send another king like David—a Messiah—who would save them from their enemies.

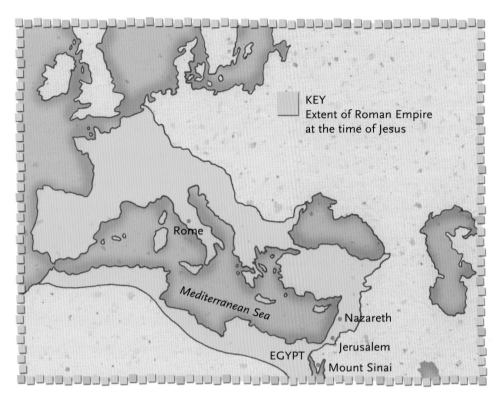

Nazareth and Jerusalem are places where Jesus spent most of his life. They were all part of the vast Roman empire around the Mediterranean Sea.

Jewish captives from Old Testament times. The Jewish people believed that God would one day send a savior to rescue them from their enemies.

## The Old Testament

The ancient writings that tell the history of the Jews and their faith in God are the Jewish scriptures. The followers of Jesus include them as the first part of their own Bible. They call them the Old Testament. The word "testament" has the same meaning as "covenant"—a reference to the covenant God made through Moses.

# 2 Learning about Jesus

Writing tools from the time of Jesus.

People today know about Jesus from the early books that were written about him: the Gospels. The four most treasured Gospels are those of Matthew, Mark, Luke, and John. It is likely that Mark's was the first to be written. It begins with these words:

*"The beginning of the good news of Jesus Christ, the Son of God."*
MARK 1:1

## Mark Introduces Jesus

Mark's Gospel then explains that another preacher, John, had burst onto the scene ahead of Jesus. John preached that people needed to turn away from their sins and repent.

## The New Testament

The Gospels of Matthew, Mark, Luke, and John are four accounts of the life of Jesus. These Gospels, along with other writings by the first followers of Jesus, form the second part of the Christian Bible. It is known as the New Testament—a reference to the new covenant Jesus explained to his followers, the disciples.

This page from a medieval copy of the Gospels shows Jesus healing a blind person. People made highly decorated books like these to show that they thought that the Gospels were real treasure.

He baptized those who repented with water in the River Jordan. He also said they needed to be ready for another prophet who would bring them closer to God.

One day, Jesus himself came to the Jordan and asked to be baptized. John did as Jesus asked. As Jesus came out of the water, he saw the heavens open and God's Spirit coming down on him in the form of a dove. He heard a voice from heaven saying, "You are my own dear Son. I am pleased with you."

Mark does not say anything about Jesus' life before this event.

## John Proclaims that Jesus Is God

John's Gospel begins with a declaration about the entire universe: everything that exists began with God's creative power. God created everything through what John calls "the Word"—God's Son.

John the Baptist dressed like Elijah, a prophet from days of old—in a tunic of camel hair tied with a leather belt. He lived in the wild country, eating the locusts and honey he found there.

*"And the Word became flesh and lived among us, and we have seen his glory as of a father's only Son, full of grace and truth."* JOHN 1:14

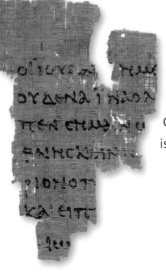

John declares that God's Son has come into the world to call people to be God's children.

This scrap of papyrus is an ancient fragment of the Gospel of John. The writing is in Greek.

# 3 Jesus' Birth: Matthew's Story

Two of the Gospels say that Jesus was born in Bethlehem. This hilltop town was famous as the birthplace of King David.

The writer of the Gospel of Matthew knew the Jewish scriptures very well. In Jesus' day, copies of those scriptures were written on scrolls and stored in pottery jars.

TWO OF THE GOSPEL WRITERS include accounts of Jesus' birth: Matthew and Luke.

## Herod and the Wise Men

Matthew's Gospel aims to show that, in Jesus, the words of the prophets recorded in the Jewish scriptures are coming true.

It begins with a list of Jesus' ancestors, including Abraham and King David, in order to prove Jesus' royal line. Then it says that Jesus' mother, Mary—through the power of God—became pregnant while remaining a virgin.

The Gospel continues with the story of wise men who saw a new star and traveled from their own countries to find the king of the Jews. First they went to the Jewish city of Jerusalem. The ruling king, Herod, was very suspicious. He asked the priests to tell him what the scriptures said about the Messiah, and they read from the book of the prophet Micah:

*"But you, O Bethlehem of Ephrathah, who are one of the little clans of Judah, from you shall come forth for me one who is to rule in Israel, whose origin is...from ancient days." MICAH 5:2*

Herod sent the travelers to Bethlehem, ordering them to bring him news of any would-be king.

The wise men found Jesus and gave him rich gifts. Then an angel warned them not to go back to Herod, so they went home by a different route.

On finding he had been tricked, Herod sent his soldiers to Bethlehem to kill all the young boys there—something, says the Gospel, that the prophet Jeremiah had foreseen.

Meanwhile, Jesus' parents, Mary and Joseph, whisked him to safety in Egypt. Later they returned to their home country—not to Bethlehem, but to Nazareth. The prophets had said, "He will be called a Nazarene."

The wise men who came to visit Jesus are traditionally shown as belonging to three different ethnic backgrounds, representing all the nations of the world.

## Gold, Frankincense, and Myrrh

Matthew simply says that the wise men brought gifts of gold, frankincense, and myrrh. Many Christians believe that the gifts are symbolic.

Gold is the symbolic gift for a king.

Frankincense is the symbolic gift for a priest—someone who will help people to worship God.

Myrrh is burial spice—a symbolic gift for someone whose death will be as important as his life.

Priests used to burn frankincense on the incense altar in the Temple. Its sweet smelling smoke was a reminder of the people's prayers rising to God.

# Jesus' Birth: Luke's Story

The angel Gabriel's announcement of Jesus' birth to Mary is often called the Annunciation.

Luke's Gospel gives the longest account of Jesus' growing-up years.

## The Birth of John

Luke begins with a story about the birth of John the Baptist. The angel Gabriel appeared to a priest named Zechariah and said that he and his wife Elizabeth would have a son who would guide people back to God.

## The Birth of Jesus

While Elizabeth was expecting her baby, something amazing happened to her cousin in Nazareth. Mary was simply looking forward to getting married to a man named Joseph. Then the angel Gabriel appeared to her and announced that God had chosen her to be the mother of a very special baby, Jesus.

"He will be great and will be called the Son of the Most High God," said the angel.

Mary was astonished, but she agreed to do as God wanted. Though a virgin, Mary conceived Jesus through the power of the Holy spirit

The baby was almost due when, months later, she traveled with Joseph to his family's home town to take part in a Roman census. As Joseph could trace his family back to King David, his home town was Bethlehem.

In crowded Bethlehem, the couple found shelter in a stable, and there Mary's baby was born. She wrapped the child in swaddling clothes and laid him in a manger.

## Jesus Is Recognized

The first people to recognize that Jesus was exceptional were some shepherds. On the night he was born, they were out on the hillside with their sheep. Angels came and said that the Savior of the people had been born—Christ the Lord. The shepherds went and found Mary and Joseph and the baby, and they believed the news they had heard.

Not long after, Mary and Joseph went to the Temple in Jerusalem for the ceremonies required after the birth. Two elderly people—a man named Simeon and a prophetess named Anna—knew they were looking at the Savior promised by God, because the Holy Spirit revealed it to them.

Luke also tells a story about the boy Jesus. When he was twelve, he went to Jerusalem with his parents for the great Jewish festival of Passover. Jesus was so eager to talk about the scriptures with the wise teachers of his faith that he got separated from his parents. They found him deep in conversation with them. It was clear that the learned men were impressed by Jesus' wisdom and understanding.

## Advent and Christmas

The celebration of Jesus' birth is known as Christmas. It is celebrated on December 25 in many churches; in others, most importantly those of the Eastern Orthodox tradition, it is celebrated on January 6.

In some Christian churches, the four weeks before Christmas are a time for remembering the Bible people and prophets who looked forward to the coming of the Messiah. This time is known as the season of Advent.

The star of David reminds Christians that Jesus was a descendant of King David. (See 2 Tm 2:8.)

# 5 Jesus' New Beginning

Jesus often used the Jewish scriptures as the starting point for his teaching.

AFTER HE WAS baptized, Jesus spent forty days in the wild country. He wanted to fast and pray about what he was going to do next. The devil tried to lead him astray.

"You are hungry," the devil said. "If you are God's Son, you can order this stone to turn into bread."

Jesus refused, quoting the scriptures: "Human beings cannot live on bread alone," he said.

The devil spoke again. "Worship me, and all the kingdoms of the world could be yours," he whispered.

"No," said Jesus. "The scripture says, 'Worship the Lord your God and serve only him!' "

A third time the devil tried to lure Jesus away from God. "Why not throw yourself down from the highest point of the Temple in Jerusalem? The scripture says that God will order the angels to keep you safe."

"No," said Jesus. "The scripture also says this: 'Do not put the Lord your God to the test.' "

After that, the devil gave up for a time.

## The Preacher and His Disciples

Jesus began to preach in the synagogues, the places where Jewish people gathered for worship on the sabbath. Most communities welcomed him, but in his home town of Nazareth, an angry crowd threw him out. Jesus then moved to Capernaum, on the shore of Lake Galilee. He chose four fishermen to help him and be his disciples: they were Simon (nicknamed Peter), his brother Andrew, and two brothers named James and John.

Later, Jesus chose eight others to join the group.

## Miracles

Jesus soon became famous for his miracles. The Gospels all say that he could heal people with just a touch. Many people flocked to him for this reason above all.

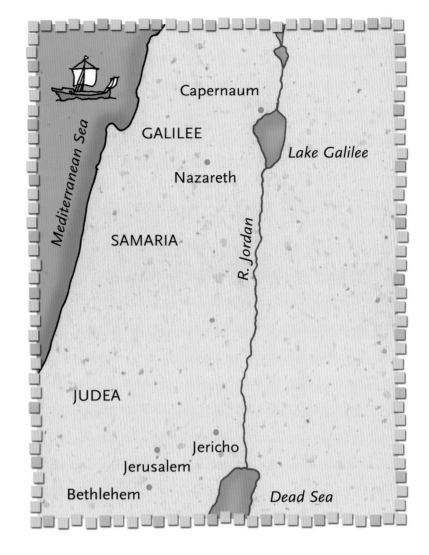

This map shows the most important places in the life of Jesus. He and his disciples spent a lot of time around Lake Galilee. The distance from there to Jerusalem was around eighty-seven miles.

## John the Baptist

John's outspoken preaching got him into trouble. He criticized the local king for marrying his brother's widow, which was against the law, and the king threw him into prison to silence him. In the end, the king's wife and her daughter plotted to have John beheaded.

John's execution was gruesome. It made Jesus very aware that his own preaching could put his life in danger.

# Jesus' Message

Jesus' close followers are called disciples, from a word meaning pupil. The names of the twelve are as follows:

• Simon Peter and his brother Andrew; • James and his brother John; • Philip and Bartholomew; • Matthew and Thomas; • James; • Simon the Patriot; • Judas (but Matthew and Mark have Thaddeus); • Judas Iscariot

JESUS PREACHED that the kingdom of God was close at hand. People needed to turn their lives around and live as God's friends. Then they would be part of the kingdom.

## Spreading the Message

Jesus knew that not everyone who listened to him would welcome his message. He often spoke in parables—stories that only some would truly understand. He likened his preaching to the work of a man who went to sow a field and scattered handfuls of seed far and wide.

Even Jesus' closest friends and helpers, the disciples, were baffled by the story, so Jesus explained it to them:

*"When anyone hears the word of the kingdom and does not understand it, the evil one comes and snatches away what is sown in the heart; this is what was sown on the path. As for what was sown on rocky ground, this is the one who hears the word and immediately receives it with joy; yet such a person has no root, but endures only for a while, and when trouble or persecution arises on account of the word, that person immediately falls away. As for what was sown among thorns, this is the one who hears the word, but the cares of the world and the lure of wealth choke the word, and it yields nothing. But as for what was sown on good soil, this is the one who hears the word and understands it, who indeed bears fruit..." MATTHEW 13:19–23*

# Parables of the Kingdom

Jesus knew that not everyone was ready or willing to understand what he meant by the kingdom of God—which he sometimes called the kingdom of heaven. He spoke to the people in parables so that only those willing to see things in a new way would understand what he was saying about God's kingdom.

## The Pearl

*"Again, the kingdom of heaven is like a merchant in search of fine pearls; on finding one pearl of great value, he went and sold all that he had and bought it." MATTHEW 13:45–46*

## The Net

*"Again, the kingdom of heaven is like a net that was thrown into the sea and caught fish of every kind; when it was full, they drew it ashore, sat down, and put the good into baskets but threw out the bad. So it will be at the end of the age. The angels will come out and separate the evil from the righteous..." MATTHEW 13:47–49*

## The Yeast

*"The kingdom of heaven is like yeast that a woman took and mixed in with three measures of flour until all of it was leavened." MATTHEW 13:33*

## The Mustard Seed

*"The kingdom of heaven is like a mustard seed that someone took and sowed in his field... [It] becomes a tree, so that the birds of the air come and make nests in its branches." MATTHEW 13:31–32*

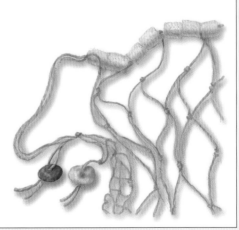

# Turn Away from Your Sins

Jesus told people to love their enemies—and even the occupying Roman troops. They could show that love by carrying a soldier's pack twice as far as they had to.

J ESUS OFTEN SPOKE directly about what it meant to live as friends of God.

## You Must Be Holy

Jesus explained that God is holy, and that those who want to be God's children must strive to be holy as well.

It was not enough simply to keep to the letter of the Law that God had given in the time of Moses. It was necessary to set one's heart on doing good even if that meant hardship and danger. "You have heard that it was said, 'Love your friends, hate your enemies,' " explained Jesus. "But now I tell you: love your enemies and pray for those who persecute you, so that you may become the children of your Father in heaven."

## You Must Forgive

The disciple named Peter once asked Jesus how many times he should forgive someone who wronged him. Would seven times be enough to meet Jesus' demands for holy living? "No," replied Jesus, "not seven times, but seventy times seven." He also said this:

*"For if you forgive others their trespasses, your heavenly Father will also forgive you." MATTHEW 6:14*

# You Must Be Humble

Jesus told a parable about two types of people whom his listeners would have recognized at once. The Pharisees were deeply religious but some of them were smug about it. The tax collectors were unpopular not only because they worked for the conquering Romans but also because most of them cheated the taxpayers to make themselves rich.

"One day two men went to the Temple to pray," said Jesus.

"One was a Pharisee. He stood apart from everyone else and said this: 'Thank you, God, that I am not greedy or dishonest or immoral like other people—like that tax collector over there, for example. Instead, I fast two days a week and give you a tenth of my income in order to show my religious devotion.'

"The tax collector hid at the back of the Temple and hung his head. 'God have mercy on me,' he said. 'I am a wicked sinner, and I know it.'

"It was the tax collector's friendship with God that was mended and not the Pharisee's," said Jesus. "Those who make themselves great will be humbled, and those who humble themselves will be made great."

The inner courtyard of the Temple where Jewish men went to say prayers.

The Pharisees of Jesus' day were proud of how they kept the Law in every detail, such as giving away a tenth of their herb crop. Jesus warned them not to forget big things, such as justice for the poor.

## The Jesus Prayer

One of the most famous Christian prayers, known as the Jesus Prayer, uses a simple version of the words said by the tax collector in Jesus' parable of the two men in the temple:

*Lord, have mercy on me, a sinner.*
*From Luke 18:13*

# 8  God's Forgiveness

JESUS CLEARLY PREACHED that people must own up to their sins, turn away from wrongdoing and choose to obey God instead. They would be forgiven and welcomed into the kingdom as God's much-loved children. The transformation was so great he once described it as being born again.

## Jesus' Power to Forgive

One day when Jesus was teaching, the Pharisees and teachers of the Law came from far and wide to listen to him. The house was so crowded that no one else could get near.

Some men came along, carrying a man who could not walk. They wanted Jesus to heal him, so they climbed the steps to the flat roof, made a hole, and let the man down on ropes, using his sleeping mat as a stretcher.

When Jesus saw how much faith they had, he said to the man, "Your sins are forgiven."

The religious leaders flashed angry, knowing looks at one another. They believed only God could forgive sins.

Olive leaves are a Christian symbol of peace and forgiveness.

This group of flat-roofed buildings shows the kind of house where a crippled man was lowered through the ceiling to Jesus.

"Which is easier to say?" asked Jesus. 'Your sins are forgiven' or 'Get up and walk'? Now I want you to know that I have authority to forgive sins."

He spoke to the man lying on his sleeping mat. "Get up and walk," he said.

The man got up at once, and made his way home, praising God.

## Jesus' Parable of the Lost Son

On one occasion, Jesus told this parable to help people understand God's love and forgiveness.

"Think of a man who has two sons," said Jesus. "The younger dreams of escaping the family farm. He demands his share of his father's wealth and goes off to squander it all on a wild lifestyle.

"Soon he falls on hard times. He takes a job looking after pigs. There, in the dust, he comes to his senses. 'I shall go back to my father and say I am sorry,' he says to himself. 'I shall beg him to hire me as a servant.'

"He sets off for home. He still has a long way to walk when his father sees him. Overjoyed, the father runs to hug him. He hardly hears the son's words of apology. Instead, he orders his servants to prepare a welcome party."

Jesus once told a parable about a lost sheep. A good shepherd, he explained, would go out into the hills to find it and bring it safely home. His joy at finding it is like the joy there is in heaven when a wrongdoer turns back to God.

Jesus' story about a father forgiving his son was intended to provide a glimpse of God's unfailing love.

# The Right Way to Live

The Temple priests were expected to help people worship God. Jesus often criticized them for making religion seem distant and difficult.

J ESUS TOLD HIS LISTENERS that they should not just turn away from wrongdoing; they should also firmly resolve to do good. Only in this way would they be able to show proper respect for God and their fellow human beings.

### Jesus' Parable of the Good Samaritan

One day an expert in God's Law came to ask Jesus a question. "Teacher," he said, "what must I do to receive eternal life?"

"Tell me what the scriptures say," replied Jesus.

The man knew the answer perfectly. " 'Love the Lord your God with all your heart, with all your soul, with all your strength, and with all your mind,' " he replied, "and 'Love your neighbor as you love yourself.' "

"You are right," said Jesus. "Do that, and you will have eternal life."

The man still wanted to test Jesus' understanding. "So who is my neighbor?" he asked. Jesus told this parable.

"There was once a man who was going from Jerusalem to Jericho. On the way, he was attacked by robbers. They took all he had and left him for dead.

"Then one of the Temple priests came by. He saw the man, but hurried past on the other side of the road.

"A Levite came by—one of the helpers in the Temple. He went over and looked at the victim, then he too hurried by."

## Goodness to Change the World

Jesus told his followers to do good for its own sake—not for public praise.

He said that those who did good would transform the world. Their shining example would be a beacon of hope in a selfish and cruel world. People would notice and they would praise God.

Mother Teresa (1910–97) was a Catholic sister who for many years worked to help the poor and destitute of Calcutta, India. She did so out of her love for Jesus and her desire for all people to love him too.

"A Samaritan—someone from the district of Samaria—happened to be using the same road. He went over to bandage the man's wounds. He helped him onto his own donkey and led him to an inn. There, he took care of him.

"The next day, he gave two silver coins to the innkeeper. 'Take care of him,' he said. 'If you spend more, I will repay you when I return this way.'"

Jesus looked at his questioner. "Which of the three was a neighbor to the man who was attacked?" he asked.

"The one who was kind to him," came the reply.

"Then you go and do the same," replied Jesus.

This ancient inn stands on the road from Jerusalem to Jericho—the setting for Jesus' parable of the Good Samaritan.

# God's Children

Jesus often taught his crowds of followers on the hills of Galilee overlooking Lake Galilee itself.

Jesus reminded his followers that the passing loveliness of flowers was a reminder of God's love and care.

JESUS PROCLAIMED that his message about the kingdom of heaven was good news.

It would be bad news if God were a frowning, critical judge who delighted in punishing wrongdoers. However, said Jesus, God is a loving Father who cares for people and wants the best for them.

## Trust in God

Because God is a loving Father, said Jesus, people must trust in God's goodness. He explained that many people spent their whole lives worrying about making money and thinking that life would be better if they could afford more things. That was a huge mistake.

"Look at the birds," he said. "They do not sow seeds or gather a harvest; yet God provides them with the food they need.

"Look at the flowers," he said. "They do not work to make clothes for themselves; yet God dresses them in petals that are lovelier than anything that the world's richest people could ever have.

"If God takes care of the birds and the flowers, you can be sure that God will take care of you. So make it your aim to live as God requires, as part of God's kingdom. God will provide you with all you need."

## "Our Father"

Jesus taught his followers to pray to God as to a loving father, using these words:

*Our Father, who art in heaven,*
*hallowed be thy name.*
*Thy kingdom come. Thy will be*
*done on earth as it is in heaven.*
*Give us this day our daily bread,*
*and forgive us our trespasses,*
*as we forgive those who trespass*
*against us. And lead us not*
*into temptation;*
*but deliver us from evil. Amen.*
*See MATTHEW 6:9–13*

This chapel stands on the place where Jesus is said to have taught his famous prayer. Each panel gives the words in a different language.

## A God Who Answers Prayer

"Are any of you fathers?" Jesus asked his listeners. "Would any one of you give your child a stone if they asked for bread? Of course not!

"How much more then will God, your Father in heaven, give good things to those who ask.

"Ask, and you will receive; seek, and you will find; knock, and the door will be opened to you."

Jesus explained that God longs to take care of everyone—as a good parent takes care of much-loved children.

# God's Power on Earth

These medical instruments date from the time of Jesus. However, few people then could afford good treatment and Jesus' miracles of healing caused joy and amazement.

THE GOSPELS TELL US that Jesus worked many miracles. These wonders were intended to show people that Jesus had power from God—power for good that was stronger than all the forces of evil.

## Power Over Illness

Jesus became famous throughout the land for his miracles of healing. Some illnesses were of the body—he cured people who could not see, who could not walk, who were sick with fever. Some illnesses were of the mind, and people who had been outcasts because of their wild behavior were able to live normally again. Jesus cured many of his own people, but he also worked miracles among non-Jews, such as the Romans. These were clear signs that God's blessings were for all people.

## Power Over Death

On more than one occasion, Jesus raised the dead to life. The young daughter of a man named Jairus was lying still and cold on her bed when Jesus came and told her to "sit up." At once, she was alive and well. A young man named Lazarus had been several days in a cold tomb when Jesus asked for the stone door to be rolled away. Jesus called to Lazarus to come out, and he came, still wearing the linen cloths in which he had been wrapped for his funeral.

These miracles were signs that God is stronger than death.

This is the entrance to the cave-like tomb where the body of Lazarus is said to have been laid.

## A World of Plenty

One day, Jesus and his disciples went to a remote place in the hope of finding rest and quiet. A crowd of five thousand people came to find Jesus, and he took the opportunity to preach to them all day. Hours went by, and Jesus knew the people would be getting hungry. However, it seemed the only food available was what a young boy had brought with him—five loaves and two fish. Jesus said a prayer of blessing and asked his disciples to share the food with the crowd. By a miracle, there was enough for them all. The scraps that were gathered filled twelve baskets.

It was a sign of God's power to meet everyone's needs.

## A World at Peace

One night, Jesus asked his disciples to sail their boat across Lake Galilee. He was tired and he fell asleep. A storm blew up—a storm so violent it threatened to drown them. Terrified, the disciples woke Jesus. He simply stood up and commanded the wind and waves to be still.

It was a sign that God is stronger than all the destructive forces at work in the natural world.

Jesus stills a storm on Lake Galilee.

This mosaic of loaves and fish in a chapel in Galilee recalls Jesus' miracle of providing food for many thousands.

# Friends of Jesus

Jesus welcomed children and said that the only way to be part of God's kingdom was to accept it as a child would.

T IME AND AGAIN, Jesus showed he valued people for who they were, not for their status. He was ready to welcome anyone into God's kingdom.

## Jesus and the Children

His disciples were slow to learn to be as welcoming as Jesus. One day, people came with their little children and asked if Jesus would bless them.

"Don't waste the teacher's time," the disciples scolded. Jesus heard them.

"Bring the children to me," he said. "The kingdom of God belongs to little ones like these."

## Mary and Martha

Jesus and his disciples spent a lot of time visiting different places, and they relied on the hospitality of local people.

One day, a woman named Martha welcomed him to stay in her home. She then busied herself with all the chores that had to be done. Her sister, Mary, simply went to listen to Jesus' teaching.

An everyday meal in Jesus' day was a pot of stew. Martha might have made this and a batch of bread for her guests.

Martha was most upset, but Jesus explained that what Mary had chosen to do was the best.

## The Cheating Tax Collector

One day, Jesus came to Jericho.

The chief tax collector there was a man named Zacchaeus. He was eager to see Jesus, but because he was a short man he could not see over the crowd.

He ran ahead and climbed a tree, and soon Jesus was right there below him.

Jesus looked up. "Come down, Zacchaeus," he said. "I want you to invite me to your house."

Zacchaeus hurried to welcome his guest. Behind him, the crowd grumbled. "Why is Jesus going to spend time with that good-for-nothing? It's not right!"

When Jesus asked to share a meal with a cheating tax collector, he showed that even outsiders could turn their lives around and be part of God's kingdom.

Meeting Jesus transformed Zacchaeus. During the meal he shared with Jesus, he stood up and made a promise: "Listen, Jesus. I will give half my belongings to the poor. If I have cheated anyone, I will pay them back four times what I took."

Jesus was pleased. "I came to find those who have forgotten that they belong to God's people," he said. "I came to bring them safely back to God."

# Who Will Follow Jesus?

Jesus' preaching about the kingdom of God called on people to change their lives. Some people felt unable to commit themselves.

Jesus said that rich people would find it hard to be part of God's kingdom. Saint Francis of Assisi (1181–1226) famously gave up all his belongings to follow Jesus. He even gave his fine clothes back to his family when he chose a life of poverty and good deeds.

## The Rich Young Man

One day, a rich young man came to see Jesus. "What must I do to receive eternal life?" he asked.

"You know the commandments in the scriptures," said Jesus. "Do not commit adultery; do not murder; do not steal; do not lie to get people into trouble with the law; respect your father and your mother."

"I've done all of that since I was a boy," said the man.

"There is one more thing," said Jesus. "Sell all you have, give the money to the poor, and then come and follow me."

"Oh," said the young man, and his face fell. "That's a lot to give up." He wandered away.

Jesus felt sad. "It's hard for rich people to enter the kingdom of God," he said. "It's easier for a camel to go through the eye of a needle!"

## The Cost of Following Jesus

Many people dreamed of following Jesus, and some promised to devote their lives to him. He warned them that they would have to give up the security of home and family.

Not everyone was ready to do so. Jesus' words on the matter were clear: "If someone starts plowing and keeps looking back, they can't do a proper job. You have to be fully committed to working for God's kingdom."

A person needs to keep their eye on the job to plow a straight furrow—or to follow Jesus.

In Jesus' day, people built watchtowers in the corner of their vineyards so they could guard their crop. An unfinished tower showed embarrassing lack of planning.

## Counting the Cost

Jesus warned people that there was a price to pay for being his followers. They could expect to face danger—the danger of being executed by crucifixion. "If you can't carry your own cross, you can't be my disciple," he said.

"Think about this: if you were planning to build something—a tower, maybe—you would have to work out the cost. Otherwise, you might get as far as laying the foundation and have to stop. People would laugh at you.

"You have to be ready to give everything up to be my disciple."

# Who Is Jesus?

JESUS KNEW THAT he had a huge following. To teach his disciples who he was, Jesus first asked them what people thought about him. "Who do people say I am?" he asked his disciples.

"Some say you are John the Baptist," they answered. "Others you say you are Elijah, the great prophet we read of in our scriptures; or perhaps another of the prophets."

"What about you?" Jesus asked. "Who do you say I am?"

Peter answered, "You are the Messiah."

Jesus ordered them not to say a word about that to anyone. He warned of hard times ahead. "I will be put to death," he said, "but I will rise again."

The snow-capped summit of Mount Hermon is where some people think Jesus' disciples saw him in a heavenly light—the Transfiguration.

## The Transfiguration

Six days later, Jesus went with Peter, James, and John to the top of a high mountain. Suddenly, the scene changed. Jesus' clothes became shining white; two prophets of olden times— Moses and Elijah—appeared and began to talk to Jesus.

Then a cloud came down and hid everything. The disciples heard a voice saying, "This is my own dear Son— listen to him."

# What Jesus Said about Himself

John's Gospel records several sayings of Jesus in which he described himself. Each saying gave a glimpse of what his life and teaching had to offer his followers.

*"I am the bread of life. Whoever comes to me will never be hungry."* JOHN 6:35

*"I am the light of the world. Whoever follows me will never walk in darkness but will have the light of life."* JOHN 8:12

*"I am the good shepherd. The good shepherd lays down his life for the sheep."* JOHN 10:11

*"I am the gate. Whoever enters by me will be saved, and will come in and go out and find pasture."* JOHN 10:9

*"I am the vine, you are the branches."* JOHN 15:5

*"I am the way, and the truth, and the life."* JOHN 14:6

*"I am the resurrection and the life. Those who believe in me, even though they die, will live."* JOHN 11:25

## The View of the Religious Leaders

The religious leaders mistrusted Jesus. For example, they claimed he was disrespectful of the Law—healing people on the sabbath and mixing with people who lived impure lives. They were also anxious about his miracles and refused to believe his power came from God.

The religious leaders criticized Jesus for his attitude toward the Law. Jesus criticized them for making a big display of being religious but doing nothing to help the poor and weak.

# Jesus in Jerusalem

Christians remember the day Jesus was welcomed into Jerusalem on the Sunday before Easter. It is known as Palm Sunday because the people waved palm branches in celebration.

THE MOST IMPORTANT FESTIVAL of the Jewish people was Passover. It recalled a key moment in their history: the time when God had helped them escape from being slaves in Egypt and made a covenant with them. Every Jew wanted to be in Jerusalem for the festival—including Jesus and his disciples.

## A Welcome Fit for a King

As they approached the city, Jesus asked his disciples to fetch a donkey so he could ride the last few miles.

The crowds of pilgrims noticed him. Suddenly, they began to cheer and wave palm branches. "God bless the king who comes in the name of the Lord," they cried.

Some religious leaders who were there were angry: Jesus was letting people welcome him as the Messiah.

## In the Temple

When Jesus entered Jerusalem, he went to the Temple. The courtyard was like a marketplace: some merchants were selling the special Temple coins pilgrims needed to make the right donations at the festival; others were selling animals for the festival sacrifices.

To everyone's surprise, Jesus began to overturn the tables. Coins jingled to the ground and ran along the flagstones. The animals broke loose and began to run. In the commotion, Jesus ordered the merchants to leave:

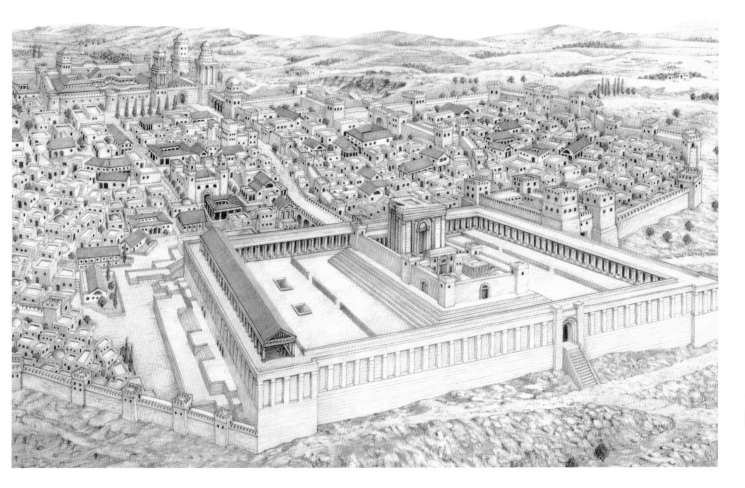

"This is meant to be a house of prayer," he cried. "You have turned it into a place for thieves."

The religious leaders were more outraged than ever.

## The Plot against Jesus

Jesus came to the Temple every day during the festival and continued to preach his message. The religious leaders wanted to silence him but they were afraid of arresting him when there were adoring crowds all around.

Then one of Jesus' own disciples gave them the chance they wanted: in exchange for thirty pieces of silver, Judas Iscariot agreed to let them know when and where they could find Jesus and arrest him quietly.

An overview of Jerusalem in the time of Jesus. On the day Jesus was welcomed by a palm-waving crowd, he would have ridden to the Temple steps and walked into the courtyard.

Judas betrayed Jesus for a purseful of silver coins.

# The Last Supper

JESUS ASKED HIS DISCIPLES to arrange the Passover meal for them all. Someone had agreed to lend them an upstairs room in Jerusalem. There they laid out the feast.

## Bread and Wine

The Passover meal was full of ceremony and meaning: the traditional food and cups of wine were used to help remember the first Passover night and the covenant that had been made between God and the Jewish people.

Jesus told his disciples to share bread and wine in memory of him. Since the first days of Christianity, believers have done so. Jesus offers his body and blood to give his followers strength on their journey to God's everlasting kingdom.

That night, Jesus began to explain the ceremony to his disciples in a new way.

*Then he took a loaf of bread, and when he had given thanks, he broke it and gave it to them, saying, "This is my body, which is given for you. Do this in remembrance of me." And he did the same with the cup after supper, saying, "This cup that is poured out for you is the new covenant in my blood." LUKE 22:19–20*

The importance of what he was saying about a new covenant did not seem to sink in. Judas Iscariot slipped away to tell Jesus' enemies where to come and arrest him. The other disciples began arguing about which one of them was the most important. Jesus said they should be looking instead for ways to serve one another.

He warned them of troubles ahead, and Peter boasted that he would stay loyal whatever the danger.

"Before dawn tomorrow, you will disown me three times," said Jesus.

When night fell, Jesus and the eleven went to a quiet olive grove known as the Garden of Gethsemane.

There, in the darkness, Jesus prayed while his disciples slept. He knew that his enemies wanted to kill him. He prayed desperately for God to allow him an easier way... but he knew that he must obey God to the end.

The Garden of Gethsemane, where Jesus spent his last night in prayer, lies just outside Jerusalem below the Temple Mount.

## A New Commandment

John's Gospel tells a different story about the last supper. Before the meal, says John, Jesus tied a towel around his waist and began washing the feet of his disciples as a servant might.

"You must serve one another like this," he explained.

After the meal, he gave them a new commandment:

*"I give you a new commandment, that you love one another. Just as I have loved you, you also should love one another."*
JOHN 13:34

Some Christians still continue the tradition of foot washing. Here, the Archbishop of Canterbury washes the feet of young Christians in a church service.

# Jesus on Trial

## Peter

Peter had promised to be faithful to Jesus. He didn't want to leave him to his enemies, but he was scared. He followed at a distance and managed to creep into the courtyard of the house where Jesus was taken. He sat by the fire there, among the servants.

A woman pointed to him. "That man was with Jesus," she announced. Peter denied it at once.

Later a man noticed him, and then another. On both occasions, Peter swore that he did not know Jesus.

A cock crowed. Peter remembered Jesus' prediction, and wept.

INTO THE SILENCE of the Garden of Gethsemane came the clatter of hurrying feet. Judas emerged from the shadows. Behind him was a crowd of men, some of them armed and ready to fight.

Judas walked straight up to Jesus and gave him the customary kiss of greeting.

"Is this how you betray me?" asked Jesus.

The armed men took charge. They hustled Jesus off to the house of the high priest.

The disciples ran away.

## Jesus and the Jewish Council

The religious leaders had organized Jesus' arrest. Next, they all met to question him.

Jesus explained they already knew all there was to know—he had preached openly.

"Are you the Messiah?" the high priest asked.

*Jesus said to him, "You have said so. But I tell you, from now on you will see the Son of Man seated at the right hand of Power and coming on the clouds of heaven." MATTHEW 26:64*

"That's blasphemy!" exclaimed the high priest. "That's using the name of God in a way that is utterly wrong. Jesus is guilty and must die."

## Jesus and Pilate

The religious leaders took Jesus to the Roman governor in Jerusalem, Pontius Pilate. They needed him to approve the death sentence.

Pilate questioned Jesus privately and came back puzzled. "That man hasn't done anything to deserve death," he said to Jesus' accusers.

By now, the religious leaders had got some of the crowd on their side. They gathered outside Pilate's residence. "Crucify him!" they cried.

Pilate was afraid of a riot—and allowing a riot in Jerusalem wouldn't be good for his career. He ordered Jesus' execution.

When Judas found out what had happened, he tried to give back the money he had been paid, but it was too late. He went and hanged himself.

Pilate asked the crowds if he should set Jesus free. "Crucify him!" they replied.

# The Crucifixion

P ILATE'S SOLDIERS MARCHED Jesus away, and all the soldiers garrisoned in Jerusalem gathered for some cruel fun. They stripped Jesus of his clothes and dressed him as a mock king, in a scarlet robe, with a crown of thorns on his head and a stick in his hand. Then they spat at him, beat him and insulted him.

Finally, they dressed him in his own clothes again and led him out to crucify him on a rocky hill just outside the city.

## The King of the Jews

When a person was executed, it was the custom to pin above them a notice stating their crime. Pilate wrote one for Jesus: "This is the king of the Jews."

The religious leaders felt anxious. "It should say, 'This man said, "I am the king of the Jews," ' " they explained to Pilate.

"What I've written stays," snapped Pilate.

Jesus hung on the cross for hours. Two criminals, one on either side, were executed at the same time. Jesus said a prayer asking God to forgive those who had plotted his death. He saw his beloved disciple standing next to his mother, Mary, and asked the young man to be a son to her. The Gospel of John says that his last words were these: "It is finished."

Many depictions of the crucifixion show Jesus' mother Mary and his beloved disciple at the foot of the cross.

## Good Friday

The day of the crucifixion is the most solemn day of the Christian year. It is known as Good Friday. Christians remember how Jesus suffered and died to save all people from sin and open to them the way to heaven.

Jesus was abused by the Roman soldiers who were ordered to crucify him. The scarlet robe, the crown of thorns, and the metal-barbed scourge are grim reminders of the cruelty he suffered.

Meanwhile, a wealthy Jewish man named Joseph, from the town of Arimathea, was already busy asking permission from Pilate to be allowed to take the body. When the soldiers were sure Jesus was dead, Joseph arranged for his body to be carried to a new tomb cut in the rock.

The crucifixion happened on a Friday, the day before the sabbath day of rest, so there was no time for the proper funeral ceremonies. Hurriedly, Joseph ordered the stone door to be rolled across the entrance to the tomb.

Jesus' crucifixion has been the most important symbol of the Christian faith throughout history. This ancient Celtic cross shows two human figures and two angels honoring Jesus' sacrifice.

# The Resurrection

JESUS' FOLLOWERS WERE devastated by his death. Not only did they no longer have their much-loved leader, but they knew that they were in danger of arrest. Even so, a small group of loyal women went to complete the funeral ceremonies as soon as they could—very early in the morning after the sabbath.

An angel tells two women the good news of Jesus' resurrection. In this picture, the tomb is shown not as a cave but as a shrine—a reminder to Christians that they worship the risen Jesus.

## The Empty Tomb

To their dismay, the women found the tomb open and the body gone. According to Luke, two men in shining clothes suddenly appeared and said these amazing words:

"Why are you looking among the dead for one who is alive? He is not here, he is risen."

The Gospels each give their own account of what happened next. Here are some of the stories.

## The Walk to Emmaus

Luke tells the story of two disciples who were walking from Jerusalem to their home in Emmaus when a stranger came alongside. They talked about the latest news— the crucifixion of Jesus. The stranger explained that everything that had happened fitted with what the scriptures said about the Messiah. The disciples were intrigued and invited the stranger to stay with them.

As he broke the bread at the beginning of the meal, they saw it was Jesus himself. Suddenly, he was gone.

## Mary Magdalene

John says that one of the women who went to the tomb was Mary from Magdala (a Magdalene). She stayed there weeping. Then two angels came and asked why she was crying. "They have taken my master away and I don't know where he is," she sobbed.

She turned around and saw another man who also asked her why she was crying. She thought he was the gardener and asked him if he had moved Jesus' body.

"Mary," said the man.

At once she recognized Jesus.

## Thomas

John says that Jesus appeared to his disciples when they were in a room together. One of the disciples, Thomas, was out at the time, and he did not believe their story.

A week later, Jesus appeared again and invited Thomas to see and touch the marks on his body. "Stop your doubting and believe," he said.

## Easter Day

The most joyful day in the Christian year is Easter Day, when Christians celebrate the fact that Jesus rose from the dead. The resurrection, as it is known, convinces them that Jesus' message is true and that those who belong to God's kingdom will not be defeated by death but have everlasting life.

Easter eggs are a part of many Easter celebrations. They are an ancient symbol of springtime and new life.

# The Followers of Jesus

This chapel is built on the site where Jesus is said to have ascended to heaven.

## Ascension and Pentecost

In the Christian calendar, the ascension of Jesus to heaven is remembered on the Thursday that comes forty days after Easter. Ten days later, Christians celebrate Pentecost Sunday and the coming of the Holy Spirit to the believers.

ACCORDING TO THE GOSPELS, Jesus told his followers to carry on the work he had begun of spreading the message about God's kingdom.

He told Peter especially to take care of all the believers in the same way that a shepherd takes care of sheep.

He told all the disciples to wait for God to strengthen them for the task ahead.

Forty days after the resurrection, the disciples saw Jesus ascend to heaven. They could only sit and wonder about what might happen next.

## Pentecost

The Jewish festival of Pentecost was held fifty days after Passover. It was another popular time for Jews from all over the empire to come to Jerusalem.

The disciples were in a room together with Mary; the doors locked against any enemies of Jesus. What happened next is told in the book that Luke wrote as a sequel to his Gospel—the Acts of the Apostles. The disciples heard a noise like a strong wind, and something that looked like tongues of fire spread out and touched each one of them.

They felt themselves changed—filled with the Holy Spirit. They rushed out into the street and began talking about Jesus in different languages.

People mocked them, thinking they must be drunk. Peter stood up and preached to them: "Each one of you must turn away from your sins and be baptized in the name of Jesus Christ, so that your sins will be forgiven; and you will receive God's gift, the Holy Spirit."

—— People who heard Peter speak on the day of Pentecost spread the news about Jesus.

—— The Christians who lived in Jerusalem were given a hard time for their beliefs. Some went off to spread their message elsewhere.

—— An apostle called Paul went on several long trips to tell people about Jesus.

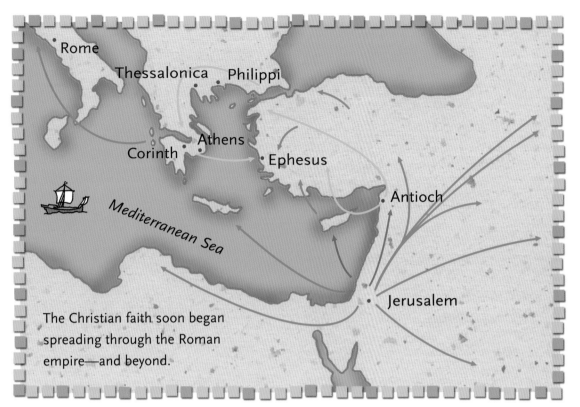

Rome

Thessalonica  Philippi

Athens

Corinth

Ephesus

Antioch

Mediterranean Sea

Jerusalem

The Christian faith soon began spreading through the Roman empire—and beyond.

On that day three thousand people believed and became followers of Jesus. It was the beginning of a faith that has lasted through the two thousand years since Jesus' life and continues to inspire millions around the world.

## Baptism

Peter baptized new believers on the day of Pentecost, and to this day, new believers continue to be baptized. Baptism marks a new beginning of life as a child of God.

The Christian faith is rooted in the life and teachings of Jesus. Its traditions have developed over two thousand years. One in three people in today's world declare themselves to be Christians, and they want their lives to show something of the love of God that was revealed in Jesus Christ.

# Index by Chapter

## A

Abraham  1, 3
Acts of the Apostles  20
Advent  4
Angel  3, 4, 19
Anna  4
Annunciation  4
Ascension  20

## B

Baptism  2, 20
Bethlehem  3, 4, 5
Bible  1, 2, 3, 4, 5, 9

## C

Capernaum  5
Children  12
Christ (*see also* Messiah) 1
Christian, Christians  1, 20
Christmas  4
Covenant  1, 15, 16
Cross, crucifixion  13, 17, 18

## D

David 1, 3, 4
Death  11
Devil  5
Disciple  5, 6, 7, 11, 12, 14, 15, 16, 17, 18, 19, 20

## E

Easter  19
Egypt  1, 3, 15
Elijah  2, 14
Elizabeth  4
Emmaus  19
Evil One  6 (*see* devil)

## F

Foot washing  16
Forgiveness  7, 8
Francis of Assisi  13
Frankincense  3

## G

Galilee  5, 10, 11
Gethsemane  16,17
Gold  3
Good Friday  18
Gospel  2, 3, 4, 5, 11, 18, 19, 20

## H

Herod  3
Holy Spirit  2, 20

## J

Jeremiah  3
Jericho  5, 9, 12
Jairus  11
Jerusalem  1, 3, 4, 5, 9, 15, 16, 17, 18, 19, 20
John (disciple)  5, 14
John (gospel writer)  2, 14, 18, 19
John the Baptist  2, 4, 5, 14
Jordan (river)  2, 5
Joseph  3, 4
Joseph of Arimathea  18
Judas Iscariot  6, 15, 16, 17
Judea  5

## K

Kingdom (of God, of heaven)  6, 8, 10, 12, 13, 20

## L

Law  1, 7, 8, 9, 14
Lazarus  11
Lent  5
Love  7, 8, 9, 16
Luke  2, 3, 4, 19, 20

## M

Manger  4
Mark  2
Martha  12
Mary (sister of Martha) 12
Mary (mother of Jesus) 3, 4, 18, 20
Mary Magdalene  19
Matthew  2, 3
Messiah  1, 3, 14, 15, 17, 19
Micah  3
Miracle  5, 11, 14
Moses  1, 7, 14
Mount Hermon  14
Mount Sinai  1
Myrrh  3

## N

Nazareth  1, 3, 4, 5

## P

Palm Sunday  15
Parable  6, 7, 8, 9
Passover  4, 15, 16
Paul  20
Pentecost  20
Peter  5, 6, 7, 14, 16, 17, 20
Pharisee  7, 8
Pontius Pilate  17, 18
Prayer  7, 10
Priest  3, 9, 17

## R

Resurrection  19
Roman empire, Romans 1, 4, 7

## S

Sabbath  5, 19
Samaria, Samaritan  5, 9
Scripture (*see* Bible)
Shepherds  4
Simeon  4
Simon  5, 6 (*see* Peter)
Solomon  1
Synagogue  5

## T

Tax collector  7
Temple  1, 4, 5, 7, 9, 15
Teresa, Mother  9
Testament  1, 2
Thomas  6, 19
Transfiguration  14

## W

Wise men  3

## Z

Zacchaeus  12
Zechariah  4